GRAND
Reflections

Grand Canyon Association

PO Box 399, Grand Canyon, AZ 86023
(800) 858-2808
www.grandcanyon.org

The Grand Canyon Association is the National Park Service's
official nonprofit partner raising private funds to benefit Grand
Canyon National Park, operating retail stores and visitor centers
within the park, and providing premier educational opportunities
about the natural and cultural history of Grand Canyon. Proceeds
from the sale of this publication will be used to support research
and education at Grand Canyon National Park.

Library of Congress Cataloging-in-Publication Data pending

Dedicated to

GRAND CANYON
NATIONAL PARK

A national park should be as sacred as a temple.

—HENRY VAN DYKE

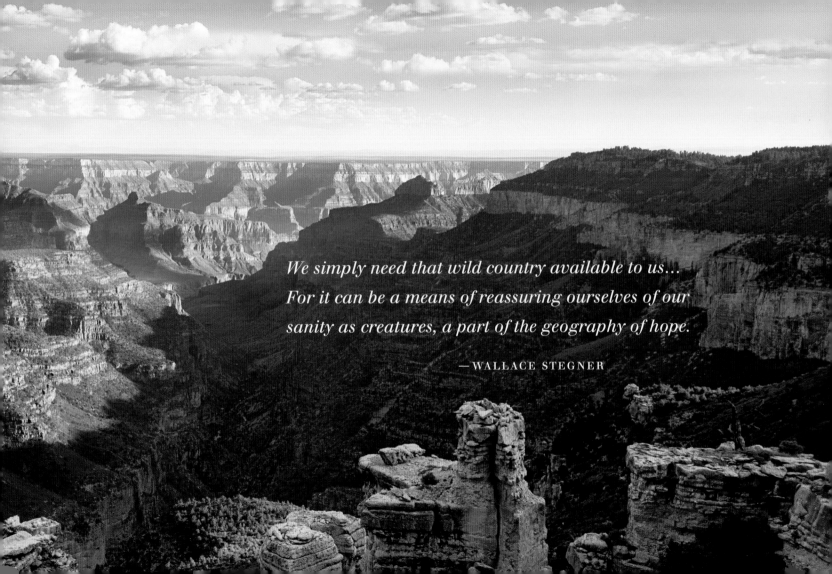

We simply need that wild country available to us...
For it can be a means of reassuring ourselves of our
sanity as creatures, a part of the geography of hope.

—WALLACE STEGNER

Most of the people who visit the parks...are impelled to visit them because of the quest for a supreme experience...the colorful chapter in the Book of Time revealed by the strata of a mile-high canyon gashed by a rushing river; the sight of strange, new plants and animals...the silence that hangs over the ruins of the habitations of forgotten peoples...these and a thousand other vivid impressions are at the heart of the experience that national park visitors travel many miles to seek...If we can remember this, we can remain true to our high calling as trustees for the greater things of America.

—NEWTON B. DRURY

May your trails be crooked, winding, lonesome, dangerous, leading to the most amazing view. May your mountains rise into and above the clouds.

—EDWARD ABBEY

12

I saw the Grand Canyon as one hears an exquisite poem, a soft strain of music on violin, cello or oboe, or sung by the human voice. … It affected one as beautiful flowers do, as the blessing of an old man or woman, as the half unconscious caress of a sleepy child whom you love.

—GEORGE WHARTON JAMES, 1910

Our kinship with Earth must be maintained;
otherwise, we will find ourselves trapped in the center
of our own paved-over souls with no way out.

—TERRY TEMPEST WILLIAMS

In the end we will conserve only what we love.

We will love only what we understand.

We will understand only what we have been taught.

—BABA DIOUM, 1968

18

It seems a gigantic statement for even nature to make, all in one mighty stone word, apprehended at once like a burst of light, celestial color its natural vesture, coming in glory to mind and heart as to a home prepared for it from the very beginning. Wildness so godful, cosmic, primeval, bestows a new sense of earth's beauty and size. Not even from high mountains does the world seem so wide, so like a star in glory of light on its way through the heavens.

—JOHN MUIR

There is nothing so American as our national parks. The scenery and wildlife are native. The fundamental idea behind the parks is native. It is, in brief, that the country belongs to the people, that it is in process of making for the enrichment of the lives of all of us. The parks stand as the outward symbol of this great human principle.

—FRANKLIN DELANO ROOSEVELT

21

Men need to know the elemental challenges that sea and mountains present. They need to know what it is to be alive and to survive when great storms come. They need to unlock the secrets of streams, lakes, and canyons and to find how these treasures are veritable storehouses of inspiration. They must experience the sense of mastery of adversity. They must find a peak or a ridge that they can reach under their own power alone.

— WILLIAM O. DOUGLAS

When your spirit cries for peace,
come to a world of canyons
deep in an old land;
feel the exultation of high plateaus,
the strength of moving waters,
the simplicity of sand and grass,
and the silence of growth.

—AUGUST FRUGÉ, 1977

We must be refreshed by the sight of inexhaustible vigor... the wilderness with its living and decaying trees, the thunder cloud and the rain... some life pasturing freely where we never wander.

—HENRY DAVID THOREAU

The whole gorge for miles lay beneath us and it was by far the most awfully grand and impressive scene that I have ever yet seen.

—THOMAS MORAN, 1873

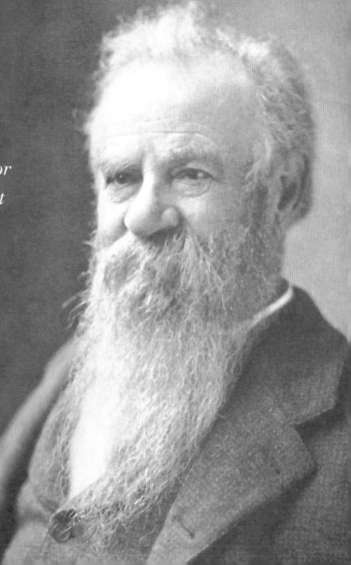

The wonders of the Grand Canyon cannot be adequately represented in symbols of speech, nor by speech itself. The resources of the graphic art are taxed beyond their powers in attempting to portray its features. Language and illustration combined must fail.

—JOHN WESLEY POWELL

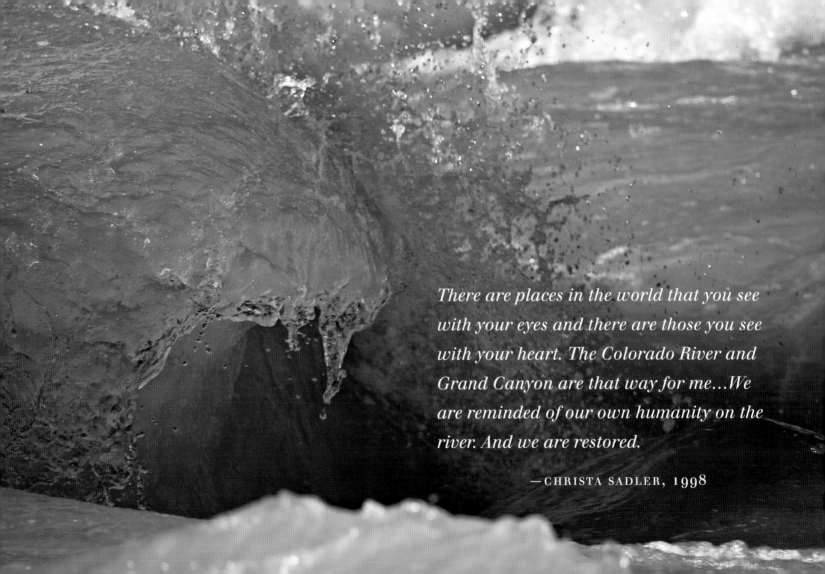

There are places in the world that you see with your eyes and there are those you see with your heart. The Colorado River and Grand Canyon are that way for me...We are reminded of our own humanity on the river. And we are restored.

—CHRISTA SADLER, 1998

A few things in the beautiful old world are too big to talk about. One can only weep before so supreme a spectacle of glory and of majesty!

— MARGARET GEHRKE

Study nature,
love nature,
stay close to nature.
It will never fail you.

— MONET

42

Earth laughs in flowers.

—RALPH WALDO EMERSON

The finest workers in stone are not copper or stone tools, but the gentle touches of air and water working at their leisure with a liberal allowance of time.

—HENRY DAVID THOREAU, 1873

Something will have gone out of us as a people if we ever let the remaining wilderness be destroyed...We simply need that wild country available to us, even if we never do more than drive to its edge and look in.

— WALLACE STEGNER

46

48

Imagine...the very heart of the world...laid bare before our eyes! ... There is nothing between you and the undertaker except six thousand feet, more or less, of dazzling Arizona climate.

—IRVIN S. COBB

In wildness is the
preservation of the world.

— HENRY DAVID THOREAU

Everybody needs beauty as well as bread, places to play in and pray in, where Nature may heal and cheer and give strength to body and soul alike.

—JOHN MUIR

55

Nature does not hurry,
yet everything is accomplished.

—LAO TZU

*In wilderness I sense the
miracle of life, and behind it
our scientific accomplishments
fade to trivia.*

—CHARLES LINDBERGH

62

The Grand Canyon of Arizona...
is wild and sublime, a thing of
wonder, of mystery; beyond all else
a place to grip the heart of a man,
to unleash his daring spirit.

—ZANE GREY, 1922

Leave it as it is. You cannot improve on it; not a bit. The ages have been at work on it, and man can only mar it...keep it for your children, your children's children and for all who come after you, as one of the great sights which every American, if he can travel at all, should see.

—PRESIDENT THEODORE ROOSEVELT, 1905

To remember that [the Grand Canyon]
is still there lifts up the heart.

—J. B. PRIESTLEY, 1935

70

Give me solitude,
give me Nature,
give me again O Nature
your primal sanities!

—WALT WHITMAN

Nature has a few big places
beyond man's power to spoil,
the ocean, the two icy ends of the
globe, and the Grand Canyon.

—JOHN MUIR

*Wilderness is not a luxury but
a necessity of the human spirit.*

— EDWARD ABBEY

Keep close to Nature's heart…
and break clear away, once in
a while, and climb a mountain
or spend a week in the woods.
Wash your spirit clean.

—JOHN MUIR

82

The parks will have a constantly enlarging, revivifying influence on our national life, for which there is no other public agency...They are our antidote for national restlessness... They are national character and health builders...They are giving a new impetus to sane living in this country.

—STEPHEN MATHER

It is never the same, even from day to day, or even from hour to hour... Every passing cloud, every change in the position of the sun, recasts the whole.

—CLARENCE E. DUTTON, 1885

No matter how far you have wandered…the Grand Canyon of the Colorado, will seem…as unearthly in the color and grandeur and quantity of its architecture, as if you had found it after death, on some other star.

—JOHN MUIR, 1898

There is something about the desert. ...This quality of strangeness... remains undiminished. Transparent and intangible as sunlight, yet always and everywhere present, it lures a man on and on, from the red-walled canyons to the smoke-blue ranges beyond.

—EDWARD ABBEY, 1968

89

There is of course no sense at all in trying to describe the Grand Canyon. Those who have not seen it will not believe any possible description. Those who have seen it know that it cannot be described...

—J.B. PRIESTLY

*Remember what
you have seen,
because everything
forgotten returns
to the circling winds.*

—NAVAJO WIND CHANT

The glories and the beauties of form, color, and sound unite in the Grand Canyon—forms unrivaled even by the mountains, colors that vie with sunsets, and sounds that span the diapason from tempest to tinkling raindrop, from cataract to bubbling fountain.

—JOHN WESLEY POWELL

96

We must maintain the
chance for contact with beauty.
When that chance dies,
a light dies in all of us.

— LYNDON BAINES JOHNSON

National parks are the best idea we ever had.
Absolutely American, absolutely democratic, they
reflect us at our best rather than our worst.

—WALLACE STEGNER

104

The national parks...should be looked upon as open books of nature, repositories of knowledge, on which every plant, herb, tree, animal, bird, insect and reptile forms a page....Life histories, habits and behavior of animals and birds should be completed in these parks, and not solely within the four walls of the schools and colleges.

—M. A. BADSHAH

The Grand Canyon is carven deep by the master hand;
it is the gulf of silence, widened in the desert; it is all time
inscribing the naked rock; it is the book of earth.

—DONALD CULROSS PEATTIE

108

The sharply defined colours of the different layers of rock had merged and softened, as the sun dropped from sight; purple shadows crept into the cavernous depths, while shafts of gold shot to the very tiptop of the peaks, or threw their shadows like silhouettes on the wall beyond. Then the scene shifted again.

—ELLSWORTH KOLB, 1914

It is a lovely and terrible wilderness—harshly and beautifully colored, broken and worn until its bones are exposed.

—WALLACE STEGNER

110

*The glories and the beauties
of form, color and sound unite
in the Grand Canyon.*

—JOHN WESLEY POWELL, 1895

114

*The Colorado was as incapable of
serenity or anger as the rocks of its
Canyon walls. ...Still the illusion
was tenacious that the river had a
will and character of its own.*

—FRANÇOIS LEYDET, 1964

Climb the mountains and get their good tidings.
Nature's peace will flow into you as sunshine flows into
trees. The winds will blow their own freshness into you,
and the storms their energy, while cares will drop off
like autumn leaves.

—JOHN MUIR

The elements that unite to make the Grand Canyon the most sublime spectacle in nature are multifarious and exceedingly diverse.

—JOHN WESLEY POWELL

121

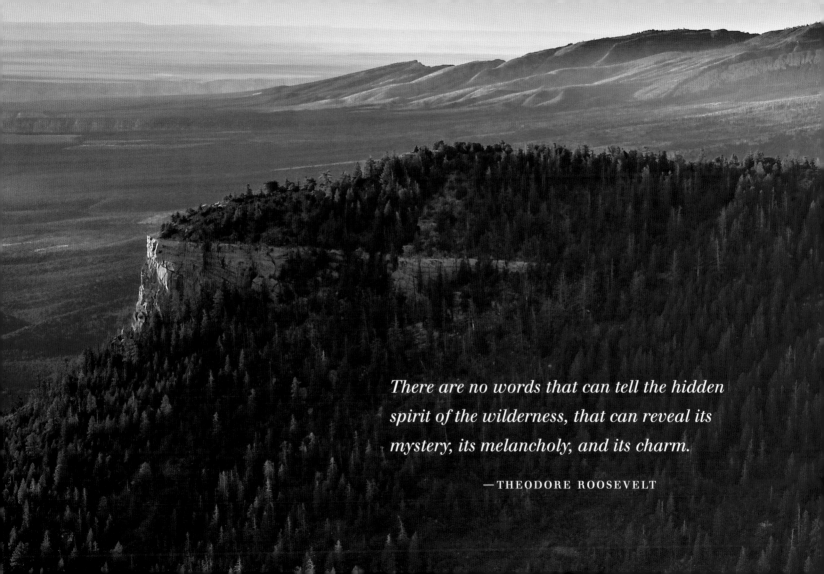

There are no words that can tell the hidden spirit of the wilderness, that can reveal its mystery, its melancholy, and its charm.

—THEODORE ROOSEVELT

PHOTO CREDITS

126